The Gift of Significance

Walking
With
People
Through
a Loss

Doug Manning

In-Sight Books, Inc.

Third Printing, 2000

Copyright © 1992 by In-Sight Books, Inc.
P. O. Box 42467
Oklahoma City OK 73123
800-658-9262
www.insightbooks.com

ISBN 1-892785-01-3

To Barbara Manning
Who gives me the gift of understanding.

INTRODUCTION

I am not an expert on grief. Grief is as unique as a fingerprint. Everyone goes through grief in their own way and on their own schedule. There can be no experts in an area with so much diversity.

I am a person who has listened to people as they told me the story of their grief. I collect the stories and share them with any group who will listen. Instead of being an expert, I am a collector and a reporter of stories.

My interest in the subject should have happened as a natural part of my being a minister. I served in that capacity for over thirty years, but somehow the need to understand grief escaped me. My involvement began when a mother demanded the right to her grief only minutes after watching her child die. That statement skinned my eyes so I could see the pain I had somehow avoided noticing.

I present to you a collection of these stories and insights framed together in what I hope is readable form.

It is my hope that these stories will share the insights and stretch the influence of some people who hurt and dared to share the hurt. Any good this book might accomplish must be credited to their account.

Doug Manning

TABLE OF CONTENTS

SECTION I
THE GIFT OF REALITY

SECTION II
THE GIFT OF SIGNIFICANCE

SECTION III
THE GIFT OF UNDERSTANDING

SECTION IV
THE GIFT OF PERSONAL CARE

SECTION I

THE GIFT OF REALITY

GENTEEL PEOPLE WANT AN ACT TO PLAY,
NOT A LIFE TO LIVE.
WE WANT ALL UNPLEASANTRIES HIDDEN
AND A TEA PARTY FOR A FUNERAL.
IS THAT TOO MUCH TO ASK?

CHAPTER I

DEATH AS PASSAGE

Americans do not do death well. We avoid talking about it and try not to even think about it. We will not use the word death if we can find any other word to use. Even the funeral homes get into the act. The rooms where dead people lie in state are called "slumber rooms." Bodies are called "remains", and the ashes left after cremation are called "cremains." Funeral directors know most people want to play the game of let's never say the word death, so they play along. George Carlin says it will not be long before we will call death a "terminal incident."

I guess we think if we do not talk about it, it will not happen. If we can avoid even thinking about it, then death will never come to our house.

Genteel people just do not talk about such things. It

may be alright to think about death late at night while no one else is around, providing we do not mention the word at breakfast.

TO OUR GOOD HEALTH

I am glad we are taking better care of ourselves and are getting more health conscious. I am glad that many have quit smoking. I am glad there are folks working to make sure that everyone who smokes will be miserable and ostracized.

I must admit that I miss the smoking section on airplanes. I used to ride there even though I did not smoke. I just met a nicer class of people in the smoking section. There were no joggers there, and no one who just quit smoking and wanted to tell me about it. Matter of fact there were very few television evangelist in the smoking section. I thought the absence of these people made it worth putting up with the smell.

I am glad many people now jog or at least walk for exercise. I am glad we are now eating better, or at least we eat better while anyone is watching. Maybe we just talk about eating healthier.

Suddenly we have health on the brain. Everywhere I look I am confronted with a new challenge to my health. The air we breathe, the food we eat, the sky overhead are all under a threat of some kind. These threats force us to health consciousness.

While I am glad for all of these wonderfully healthy advances in our world, I must say that some of this comes from our obsessive fear of death. That which comes from this fear is not healthy. Our fear of death may well be doing us more harm than good eating habits and exercise can offset.

It seems to me we will eat anything if someone says it will make us live a little longer. The experts have us eating oats now. They will have us grazing next.

I am so tired of hearing about cholesterol, I could die. I want to ooze cholesterol for three days when I die. I want them to mark off my grave and tell folks to watch where they step or cholesterol will come right up through their shoes.

I do not intend to jog. My theory is that people who jog either die while they are jogging or they live long enough to drive their children crazy. I have no intention of doing either of these.

Most of this is said in jest of course, but the fears are real. It makes me want to shout, "The death rate is one each!" "The leading cause of death is life!" In spite of our obsessions and our avoidance and our denials, we will die.

THE BASIS OF FEAR

Our fears are really quite natural. From a very early age we were programed to believe anything connected with death was eerie and mysterious. We were taught to hold our breath while the car drove past a cemetery. Walking through the cemetery at night was an invitation to being confronted by some ghost. The fear of death is deeply ingrained in us.

Death is an unknown, and it is natural to fear the unknown. I can't relate to anyone who says they have absolutely no fear of death. Since I do not know very many people who have died and then recovered, I am going to be afraid. The best I can hope for is that the fear will not become obsessive and dominate my life.

We do not want to talk about death because we do

not want to think about it. Often we think about it whether we want to or not. A sudden thought flashes through our minds, and we wonder for a moment what is on the other side. Most of the time we can turn it off and go on to other thoughts.

FEAR OF INTIMACY

The fear of death is more than just fearing the thought of dying. A great deal of our reluctance to face death is a fear of intimacy. Talking about death is the ultimate intimacy. These are feelings that are not found anywhere else on earth. Many of us do not handle intimacy very well. We are afraid of situations where we might lose control. We are not comfortable with emotions running loose. The first time a tear appears, we want to run.

Our defense against having to deal with intimacy is to put on a stoic front and avoid talking about anything that can create an intimate setting. We become like little boys avoiding the kissing scenes in the movies.

Some of our fear comes from not knowing what to say to people in pain. The most verbal among us can become dumbstruck in the presence of pain or death. So we avoid any contact with death. At least we avoid any conscious contact. We still face it late at night.

It is strange, but we seem to have a fascination with death while trying to avoid the subject. The popularity of horror movies indicates that, while we try to avoid death in real life, we are drawn to it like moths to the flame. We just want it on a screen with the reality diminished.

I think we desperately need a new concept of death. Our obsessions and fears bring on much harm. found a parable that gave me a new concept a few months ago. I have looked for the author and have hit dead ends every time. I have heard it came from a Catholic diocese in California, but I have been unable to verify the source. It puts death in the perspective we need.

The Parable of the Twins

Once upon a time, twin boys were conceived in the same womb. Weeks passed, and the twins developed. As their awareness grew, they laughed for joy: "Isn't it great that we were conceived? Isn't it great to be alive?"

Together, the twins explored their world. When they found their mother's cord that gave them life, they sang for joy: "How great is our mother's love, that she shares her own life with us!"

As weeks stretched into months, the twins noticed how much each was changing. "What does it mean?" asked the one. "It means that our stay in this world is drawing to an end," said the other. "But I don't want to go," said the other one. "I want to stay here always." "We have no choice," said the other. "But maybe there is life after birth!" "But how can there be?" responded the one. "We will shed our life cord, and how is life possible without it? Besides, we have seen evidence that others were here before us, and none of them have returned to tell us that there is life after birth. No, this is the end."

And so the one fell into deep despair, saying, "If conception ends in birth, what is the purpose of life in the womb? It's meaningless!

Maybe there is no mother after all?" "But there has to be," protested the other. "How else did we get here? How do we remain alive?"

"Have you ever seen our mother?" said the one. "Maybe she lives only in our minds. Maybe we made her up, because the idea made us feel good?"

And so the last days in the womb were filled with deep questioning and fear. Finally, the moment of birth arrived.

When the twins had passed from their world, they opened their eyes and cried for joy. For what they saw exceeded their fondest dreams.

THE COST OF FEAR

If we could see death as passage into life it would make a profound difference. We could talk about it with openness and honesty. We could face it and prepare ourselves emotionally for the reality. We are not prepared to live until we can accept the fact of death. When we realize that life lasts for a limited time, then we can get on with the business of living each day to the maximum.

Our reluctance to face death keeps us from making some wonderful discoveries. Elizabeth Kubler-Ross's studies now let us know that death may be passage into life. In his play, LAZARUS LAUGHED, Eugene O'Neill has Lazarus coming out of the grave laughing. When asked about the other side all he would say is; "It is all life, nothing but life."

The fear of death has a profound effect on our lives. It also has a profound effect on how we handle the death of a loved one and on how we try to help others face a death. I think the fear of death robs us of some healing traditions: The fear of death and the reluctance to talk about dying means most of us will die alone.

The avoidance of death can cause us to miss closure and reality when they are the most needed and the most available.

The fear of death and the reluctance to talk about it can cause people to miss the natural process of grief.

The fear of death and the reluctance to talk about it can keep us from establishing the significance of the person who has died. I think significance is an undiscovered key to healing after a loss.

CHAPTER II

THE RITUALS OF DYING

A physician said, "No one dies of old age anymore." I asked what he meant, and he explained. "We will not accept old age as a cause of death. People must die of a disease with a name no one can pronounce, after a tremendous battle with extraordinary methods trying to keep them alive. We just will not let someone die of old age."

The physician opened up a can of worms I hesitate to deal with in this book. At some time we must face the ethical dilemma of how to relate to terminal illness. The issue we need to face in this book is that our fear of death makes it difficult for us to allow others the chance to deal with their deaths. We tell terminally ill people they may recover when they are moments away from death. We do not know what to say or how to act in these cases, so we avoid the subject altogether.

There was a time when we allowed people to have the rituals of dying. My grandfather died while still a young man. Something poisonous bit him, and since modern medicines were not available, he died in a period of a few days. No one tried to tell him he was not going to die. He had a special time with each of his children. He called them one by one to his side, and they talked about his dying. That allowed him the rituals of dying. Dying rituals allow people the chance to work through their feelings and prepare for the passage.

Now we debate whether or not people should be told the truth about their condition. Dying people know they are dying. There are too many clues for them not to know. The whispered conversations in the hall, the presence of concerned friends, overly kind nurses, and the signals given by body language are too evident for the condition to be a secret. Terminally ill people know they are dying. The issue is not whether they should know. The issue is do we dare face it with them.

The first time I ever allowed a person to talk about their dying, I had to force myself to stay in the room. I was not raised in a world of intimacy. I did not know how to handle feelings. I would stand at the door and throw scriptures at sick people, or I would say a prayer and leave at the slightest indication that feelings were about to surface. If someone said, "I am not going to make it." I would immediately say, "Oh yes you are; you look better than you have in weeks. You have good color." I liked to talk about color. I have told people they had good color when they looked as white as snow.

One day a lady said she was not going to make it, and I asked if she wanted to talk about it. When she said she did and then started to do so, I had to hold the chair with both hands in order to stay in the room. But I did stay. And I learned the value of allowing people the chance to deal with their dying. Since that time, some of the best experiences of my life have happened while helping people face their passage. Dying rituals happen when people are allowed to talk and someone listens.

TALKING PREPARES

Most dying people want to talk about their death. There are exceptions, and my father was one of them. The closer he came to death the less he talked. Some people cannot say goodbye, so they divorce themselves and use silence to avoid the pain of leaving. My father grew silent. My brother also died in silence, so I may do the same. It may be genetic.

Most dying people will choose a person to be the one they want to talk with about their death. A friend of mine was dying and he chose me. He asked his wife to send for me. She knew what he wanted to talk about and she wanted the discussion to happen, but she just could not let it take place. When we tried to talk, she could not leave the room, and he would not talk with her there. She was afraid if the talk happened he would die, so she could not let it happen. The wife and I would discuss the need, and she would promise that next time she would leave the room, but then she just couldn't.

I tried one more time during the noon hour one day. The whole family was there, so we could not talk. He died at two o'clock that afternoon. I was devastated. I did not get to help my friend face his death.

I went to the hospital. Family members were in the hall waiting for the funeral director. I decided I would go into the room and stay with him until the funeral director arrived. If I could not help him die, I at least could stay by his side as long as possible.

A housekeeper stood near him in the room. Evidently she stayed there because she too wanted to be with my friend.

"Did you have some talks with my friend," I asked.

"Yes," she said.

"Did you talk to him about dying?" I asked.

When she said she had, I almost kissed her. I had no chance for a private talk with him, but she had fulfilled the need.

Since that time I have discovered that the caregivers who most often talk to the terminally ill are the house-keepers and nurses' aides. They work late at night, when the patients often have a hard time sleeping and want to talk. The housekeepers and aids are not permanent members of the family, so they are easy to talk to. They provide a wonderful service that no one else seems to want to do. They give the patient the right to talk about dying, and talking about dying is the best way to prepare for and face death.

TALKING ALLAYS FEARS

I received a call from a nursing home asking if I could help with a hysterical lady. I did not know the lady, and she could not talk. She had a disease that affected her vocal cords, and all her communication had to be written on a child's magic slate. Somehow we overcame the barriers and began to communicate. I asked her what she was afraid of.

"Death," she wrote.

My ministerial instinct almost took over, and I started to pull out all of my devotional material about life after death. Instead I asked, "Are you afraid of death, or are you afraid of dying?"

She wrote, "Dying."

Somehow we communicated that she was obsessed with the fear of choking to death.

I asked, "Do you want me to find out how you are going to die?"

She immediately wrote, "Yes."

I asked if she wanted me to tell her the truth when I found out.

Again the answer was yes.

I contacted her physician and found out she would indeed choke, but she would be in a coma long before the choking began.

I shared the news with her, and followed her for two years until she died. She was never again in panic about her dying. She found someone who would tell her the truth, and the truth really did "set her free."

TALKING GIVES PERMISSION

A lady chose me as the one to talk with concerning her death from cancer. It was another case of the family wanting the talk to happen, but being unable to let it happen. The husband would send for me, and then stand by the bed to prevent her from talking — and perhaps from getting ready to die in the process.

We were in her hospital room, and the husband was busy talking to a visitor. The lady pulled me close and said, "I am just so tired."

"Are you saying you want to let go?" I asked.

She did not answer but said, "Well, I have those grandchildren." She had raised her grandchildren.

"You did a great job in raising the grandchildren, and

the raising will pay off." I said. "They are grown and are going to be fine. If you want to go, it is okay."

She pulled me closer and kissed me. In two hours she was dead. She just needed permission.

THE GIFT OF BEING HEARD

All of this is dying ritual. Basically, dying ritual is the chance to talk and be heard. Being heard is all people need, but that may be the hardest thing for them to find. No one wants to talk to people about their dying.

That is the genius of Hospice. Hospice programs involve many things of course, but one thing that makes them special to me is that they are committed to putting someone beside the bed who will allow people to talk about dying. The ultimate intimacy is to talk with someone about death. These folks willingly walk into the ultimate intimacy.

The first "hospice call" I know anything about was on the mount of transfiguration when Moses and Elijah came to talk to Jesus about his death which would happen in Jerusalem. That was hospice.

A rabbi heard me make that statement and said, "No, that was just three Jews facing reality."

I will accept that also.

The most poignant picture of the need for hospice is the crucifixion. Not from any religious point of view, but just from the standpoint of watching someone struggle with their dying, Jesus said some things in the process of his dying. Ministers have made these into some kind of theological statement (as they may well be), but behind the theology is a man facing death with no one to hear his pain or his fears.

He wanted to talk about his family, and there was no

one, so he turned to a man and said, "Take care of my mother." That was not adequate.

He wanted to talk about how he felt about the people, and there was no one, so he said, "Forgive them; they do not know what they are doing." That was not adequate.

He wanted to talk about his pain, and there was no one to talk to, so he said, "I thirst." Need I say that was not adequate?

He wanted to talk about how it felt to die alone, and all he could do was scream, "My God, why have you forsaken me?"

He wanted permission to die, and there was no one to give it. All he could say was, "It is over." Not adequate, not adequate indeed.

And yet we let people die in loneliness and fear because our own fear of death will not let us face the ultimate intimacy and give people dying rituals.

CHAPTER III

THE RITUALS OF REALITY AND CLOSURE

I spoke at my brother's funeral. I did not want to do so. I do not think ministers are wise to place themselves in a position that demands intense control and denial.

The family assumed I would speak, so no other arrangements were made. If I had refused to speak, then no one would have spoken.

After the service a woman said, "That must have been one of the hardest things you have ever had to do." I did not want to get into a discussion, so I said it was. In fact, it was one of the easiest things I have ever done. I wished it had been hard.

The service was designed to hide the fact that anyone had died. We gathered to go along with that design. My mother sat through the service without shedding a tear. It was a time for suppression of all feelings and denial of death.

Tom's death came after a six month battle with cancer. Six months is almost sudden death to a person who had always been healthy. We were able to keep him at home until the last moments of his life. When death came, we followed his wishes, and he was removed and immediately cremated. It was as if he died and was no more.

Several days after his death and cremation, a brief memorial service was held in the chapel of the military base where he served. We allowed thirty minutes for the service and the military honors, and then adjourned to the officer's club for cocktails.

The cocktail time was typical of all cocktail parties. Somehow I thought cocktails after a funeral would be different, but there was no difference. We made small talk to avoid the subject of death. I wondered when we were going to get to act like something had happened. When would it be proper to cry? When would it be proper to admit that Tom died? It was never proper at this event. Tom died February 8, 1990. The proper time for mourning has not yet arrived more than a year later.

I watched the family and realized their need for reality and closure was not going to be met. My fear was that the lack of reality would have an adverse effect on the grieving process. I think my fears have been realized. Most of the family have had a difficult time facing the reality of the death. The grieving process has been slow to develop. The need for significance has been more difficult to establish and maintain.

We left the chapel with unfinished agendas. The whole atmosphere seemed unreal. No one knew what was proper to feel or to express. I remember hearing my mind repeat the word "inadequate" over and over. Our efforts at memorializing him seemed inadequate in every way.

I was especially concerned for one son. He had been with his father a great deal during the illness and was present when his father died. People say they want to remember their loved ones as they were, but this son's remembrance of his father has to be one of a man struggling for his last breath.

The experience had a lasting effect on me. If this is the wave of the future in funerals then we must get ready for some long term negative repercussions. To deny death is to delay the process of healing. Facing death is painful and certainly not neat or pleasant, but it is one of the necessities in healing. Tom meant well, but we do not do our loved ones a favor by protecting them from all unpleasantness.

Tom planned his funeral. He made each plan with the idea of protecting his family. He did not like funerals. Funerals are a strange subject for discussion between brothers, but we often talked about our likes and dislikes about funerals. Tom's military career made him aware of death, and his last tour of service required him to be the officer who helped families make funeral arrangements. Since I served as a pastor for thirty years and have written on the subject of grief, it became natural for us to discuss this unusual subject.

We never agreed on the subject. That may be the reason Tom brought it up so often. He knew I would rise to meet his objections, and a lively discussion would ensue. Tom did not use the usual arguments about funerals. His concerns did not fit the pattern. Most of the time those who object to funerals talk about how much they cost. Ever since the early sixties when Jessica Mitford wrote a book that was critical of the cost of funerals, that has been the major objection to funerals. Tom was involved with the cost almost daily, but it seemed to him that funeral homes were receiving fair pay for services rendered. He did not see the funeral director as a money-grubbing leech. He recognized them as professionals doing a hard job well. Our conversations were deeper than cost, and much harder for me to rebut.

Tom liked funeral directors, he did not like funerals. His dislike was directed more to the clergy than anyone else. He did not like the impersonal sermons he heard. He complained that we clergy persons were more intent on conversion than on comfort. His criticism burned at first. After being out of the ministry for several years, I have found that clergy get more criticism about funerals than almost any other area. Much of this criticism is undeserved. Hopefully this book will give some ways to reduce this criticism.

Tom thought the funeral music was awful. He wanted them to play "Oklahoma" at his funeral. I tried to tell him that was possible, but somehow he could not believe it.

His harshest criticism was reserved for the practice of viewing the body. He thought this was a pagan fetish that should be abolished. His decision to be instantly cremated was to prevent anyone from seeing him in a casket.

Our friendship was a miracle of sorts. Tom was an all-state football player who became a jet pilot. I was a terrible athlete who became a Baptist preacher. Somehow he came down off his pedestal and we became friends. Matter of fact, we became best friends. We called about once per week and spent as much time as possible together. I knew him and he knew me. I knew enough about him to know that the things he said about the funeral were not the real issues. He used these complaints to hide the real issues.

Behind the criticism was the fact that he felt the need to protect himself from the intimacy of dealing with death, and the need to protect his family from any pain or discomfort at his passing.

Being an ex jock and an officer in the military provided enough qualifications for a man to be afraid of intimacy. Tom did not express feelings very well. He could be the perfect stoic. Even when he was facing the final battle with cancer, he could not talk about how he felt, nor how he feared. He went, as they say, "like a man"— whatever that means.

 He really thought if the family did not see him they would not grieve as much. If they did not see him, they would not have to face the fact of his death. He could just slip away and be no more. He was honest in this concern. To him, they would be better off if they did not face it. They would be better off if they could deny. He was going to help them in this effort.

He could never grasp the need for reality in the face of death. To him, reality would take care of itself. The important thing, as he saw it, was to go through the death and funeral as easily as possible. He thought my insistence on reality was adding pain to pain.

REALITY HEALS

Asking people to face reality at death seems to be rather harsh treatment of an already hurting person. On the surface it would seem much better if they did not have to go through anything else. They are hurting enough already without our insistence on facing reality. At a time like this isn't it more humane to leave them alone and shelter them from every storm?

It may seem better, and for the moment it is less painful. However, in the long run the pain we face after a death can motivate us to reconstruct our lives. It hurts, but people need reality. They need closure.

I discovered the meaning of the word closure in a college classroom in Dallas. I was speaking about the need for reality, and a student said, "You are talking about closure." I asked her to explain, and she told her story.

"My mother died three years ago. I was going to remember her as she was, so I did not see her after her death. I would not go to the funeral home and barely went to the funeral. I would not allow myself to think about her or her death. I never did deal with her death until the night I graduated from high school. I was walking across the stage to receive my diploma and happened to see my father in the audience. Dad was sitting next to an empty chair, and my mother's death hit me. I fell apart right there on the stage. A few months ago my grandmother died. I went to see her body in the funeral home, and it gave me closure. I dealt with her death."

I think it is very important for the family to view the body. I do not have an opinion about other people viewing and think that is a matter of personal choice, but I am most adamant about the value of the family having this time of closure. I think it has positive effects on their future health and well-being.

Almost every time I speak on this subject someone thinks I am against cremations. I am not against cremation to any degree at all. I just think the body should be prepared, and the family have a time of closure before the cremation happens. I believe immediate removal and cremation can cause emotional damage. There is too much denial and avoidance involved for there to be good emotional health in this process. Since some areas of the United States are now experiencing instant removal and cremation in forty percent of the funerals, a growing number of unhealthy funerals is occurring.

I think the family should see the body even when it might not seem appropriate for them to do so. At times this is impossible of course, but I now think they should see what they can see. If all there is to see is one foot, then show them the foot.

I worried about that statement until a nurse told me a story. This nurse is a pioneer in the area of allowing parents of stillborns and miscarriages the opportunity to see, hold, and memorialize the baby.

In the past we tried to act as if these children were not really children, and their deaths did not matter. Thanks to people like this nurse, we now see the healing effect of allowing the families to bond and grieve over such deaths.

The nurse had her theories put to the test. A stillborn had a disease that caused the face to disintegrate. The father said he wanted to see the child. The nurse was not sure that would be a good idea in this case. The baby did not even look human. The doctor told the nurse to put the face together and show it to the father.

The father looked at the stillborn child and said, "Well, it has my wife's eyes!"

That is all he saw. Several months later the nurse was talking to the father and said how much she worried about showing the baby to him. She told the father that she was afraid the baby looked too bad for him to see.

He said, "You remember the baby as looking bad; all I can remember is she had my wife's eyes.

The need for closure can be seen in the lives of those whose loved ones have been missing in action since the Viet Nam war. For twenty years these folks have had an open end to their lives. It is a haunting experience for them, and they find it difficult to move from expecting the return of the person to finding comfort in the memories. There has been no closure.

The business manager in my office had a son who committed suicide three years ago. Justin was a wonderful young man who fought illness all of his life— much longer than I would have had the courage to fight. He laid his plans well, and placed a gun to his temple one afternoon. I happened to be in town and got to the house shortly after his mother. The mother was headed into the bedroom where Justin lay. I stopped her and said, "I don't think you want to go in there."

"I want to see him," she said.

"You can see him this evening," I responded. I hoped I was right.

"I don't want to see him in a casket," She said.

I promised he would be on a bed and she agreed to wait.

The funeral director did a remarkable job. That night we were able to gather the family around Justin and begin the process of closure. I do not know what the funeral director charged for his work. I do not care. It was more than worth the cost. We started the long process of healing standing beside his bed that night.

I often hear such statements as, "I want to remember the person as they were, not laid out in some casket." That statement might be fine if the person making the statement is not one of the immediate family. Remembering them as they were only works if we do not have to see the person after they become ill. People do not die pretty except in the movies. Family members who stand and watch a loved one die by inches need something to remember besides the scenes lived through beside the bed.

I stood beside my father through the eight months of his dying. I cannot begin to say how grateful I am that my last view of him was not the moment of his death. The skill of the embalmer means I remember him looking very much like he was before his illness. I needed to see him as he was when he was alive, not how he had deteriorated in the process of dying.

The process of memories is made smoother when there has been closure and reality. Denial is an enemy to the grief process. Denial at the funeral home leads to denial at home. It would be nice if we could go on and act like there is no death and no pain. It would be nice if we could just forget and go on. It would be nice, but it would not be healthy. Healthiness happens when we face and grow through, instead of avoiding and denying.

Denial leads to fantasizing. I have a friend whose son was killed in a plane crash. He had no chance for closure. He received an urn with what they said were his son's remains. He could not find a way to face the death. His fantasies became so real he thought his son had escaped the crash and was lost in the mountains near the crash site. He hired planes to search for his son. His process of moving toward memories has been painfully slow and painfully evident.

People who fantasize through the grieving process are much more prone to internalize the anger when it comes. The lack of reality leaves them with nothing concrete for the anger to focus upon. Anger with no focus usually turns inward, and they are left thinking the death was somehow their fault. This can prove to be devastating to those already crushed by grief.

THE DIFFERENCE BETWEEN
IMAGINATION AND MEMORIES

There is a difference between imagination and memories. In death, that which we leave to the imagination returns to do damage. This is especially true with children. Our efforts to protect children leave them with nothing to hang onto except imagination. Imagination in children means they will jump to their own conclusions as to the cause of the death. Often they conclude the death was their fault.

"This happened because I was mad and wished this person would die." Or "It happened because I wet the bed." There is no telling where a child's imagination will lead.

It may be somewhat traumatic for a child to view the body of a loved one. It is much more traumatic when our efforts at protection result in the child being excluded and lost in the shuffle. The child will try to find out what is happening. The choice is whether they find out the truth or what their imaginations can create.

Using double talk to avoid answering children's questions may leave them traumatized and confused. We use double talk because we can not say the word death. We tell a child the person went to sleep, and then wonder why the child is afraid to go to sleep. Or we tell them Jesus took the person because He loved him, and then expect the child to sing Jesus loves me in Sunday School. We must learn to be comfortable enough with the fact of death to face it without leaving room for imagination to do its work.

This was brought home to me in graphic form by Justin's mom. A few months after Justin's death she told me she was going to do something that I might not agree with. She was going to go to the police and get the pictures they took of Justin in the room where he shot himself. I did not understand and asked her if she was sure she wanted to see him like that. I do not know anything about guns, but Justin put a 357 Magnum to his head and pulled the trigger. That sounds like a cannon, and I had seen the results. When I began to explain the situation she said, "I know all of that, but you see those pictures cannot possibly be as bad as my imagination has made it. I have spent these months hearing hints of his head being blown off, and I have a picture in my mind that must be erased."

She saw the pictures. A few months later I asked her what seeing the pictures had done. She said, "I cannot tell you how relieved I am. He looked bad, but not anything like as bad as my imagination had made it."

If the choice is between reality and pain or imagination, choose reality and pain, even if the choice involves a child.

CHAPTER IV

THE RITUALS OF GRIEF

At a seminar in New England a lady shared one of the unforgettable stories in my collection. She and her mother were in a car wreck when she was eight years of age. Her mother was killed, and she was unconscious for several days. When she awoke the funeral was over, and the family was trying to return to normal life. No one ever said a word to her about her mother. No one asked her if she remembered the accident. No one let her talk about her feelings.

When she returned to school a classmate said, "Was your mother really killed?"

When the lady told us the story she said, "It felt so good to talk about mother. It was as if a dam broke and floods of feelings came out. It hurts to talk and remember, but it hurts much more to remember and not talk. "

This lady's story could be reinforced by many others with similar accounts. People try not to talk about death and dying. They especially try not to talk to children about death and dying. We avoid talking because we believe in some of the myths about grief our society has created.

Myth 1
It hurts to remember.

We need to help them forget. We should not "bring it up" because that will open up old wounds.

People are going to remember whether we "bring it up" or not. Grief is not a process of forgetting, it is a process of learning to cope while we remember.

Myth 2
Grief is an enemy to be avoided.

A woman told me her best friend had suffered the death of a child. She had avoided the friend ever since the death. She said, "The child that died was my daughter's best friend, and I have not told my daughter about her friend's death. "

I asked her why she had not done so.

She said, "Well, won't that make my daughter grieve?"

"If you are lucky it will," I responded. "Grief is a friend that heals us of hurt, not an enemy to be avoided at all cost. Would it not be better for your daughter to face the death of a friend and grieve through the loss rather than never know what happened and have to reach her own conclusions? Most of the time a child will conclude they caused the friend to go away. "

Grief is a positive force for healing, not something to be feared and avoided.

Myth 3
If we do not talk about it, grief will go away.

Unresolved grief is the cause of some of the major social problems we face. That seems like a strange statement since we see no connection between grief and social problems. We have no way of knowing how many of the things we call social problems have their beginning in grief or trauma that has not been properly handled. Grief that is left to fester often exemplifies itself in some of the things we call social problems.

We cannot determine how much divorce comes out of grieving. We know the divorce rate increases dramatically among couples who have suffered the death of a child. We would expect just the opposite to happen. It seems logical to expect a couple who has suffered the death of a child to be drawn closer as they suffer together, and would come through the experience with a stronger relationship.

The reality is that the couple will usually go through grief on a different schedule and with different expressions of their feelings. The female is more likely to enter her grief almost immediately, while the male tends to hold back and avoid. The couple is in such pain they do not have very much to give to each other, and yet they expect the other person to take away the pain. These differences and expectations can drive wedges between the couple that can lead to a divorce. The divorce usually happens several years later, so we may not see the connection between the grief and the divorce.

There is no way to determine how much substance abuse comes from unresolved grief. I conducted a funeral for a man whose wife had shot him. It was a strange experience to say the least. We had to wait until the wife was released from jail before we could plan the funeral. She participated fully in the funeral, and everyone seemed to accept her presence as normal.

We accepted this unusual participation because we know the lady is a medical victim. She has always thought if one pill would help, what would three do? She sits in a restaurant in our town every afternoon, and it is evident she has very little idea that she shot her husband. She was acquitted at the trial because no one thought she was aware enough to be responsible. We all think her condition is pitiful. What we do not recognize is that her addiction started twenty-one years ago when her son was killed in a car crash.

Myth 4
Sympathy makes it worse.

If we sympathize with people they will never get over their grief.

The truth is sympathy—real sympathy—is based on understanding. Understanding is one of the great healing words.

We maintain these myths because we need them. We fear facing death and our own mortality. We try to make believe these unpleasantries do not exist. It seems to me this is especially true among the affluent. We want to play the game of the good life. There seems to be a need to see life as a tea party. If death happens, then cover it quickly and pour the tea.

I passed out in a restaurant while eating dinner with some friends. As soon as I fell, one of my friends, whom I had known all of my life, jumped her chair sideways so her back was to the scene and tried to carry on a conversation. We have laughed about this incident many times and tried to understand the almost instinctive reaction that caused her to turn her back. The reason is we just do not want to deal with anything that makes us face the fact that there is pain and sorrow in this world. We want to pour the tea.

The result is that people are left to grieve in silence while friends and loved ones go back and play wonderful life.

We also avoid because we do not know what to say to people in pain. A man grabbed me as I walked into the hospital recently.

"You must help me," he said. "My friend is in this hospital dying of cancer, and I have been out here for two hours walking the floor, trying to get enough courage to go into the room. Tell me what to say to my friend. "

I told him he did not have to say anything. His presence mattered more than any words. I think I frightened him even more. He wondered how he could just be there and not say something, and how that could possibly help.

We have learned most of the things we know about grief in the last ten years. In 1978 when I first wrote about grief, I read every book I could find on the subject. That totaled three books. Today there are libraries full of books on the subject. Most of what we have learned has come from listening to those who are walking through the process of grieving. Studying grief remains a difficult task from a strictly clinical viewpoint. Since it is an emotion, and since it is an individualized experience, we are left with knowledge from experience as our major source.

We may be over studying the subject. If we are not careful we will stereotype the experience and try to force everyone to grieve in a set plan and a set schedule. After years of listening to the subject, it seems to me there are a few basic concepts we need to understand.

GRIEF IS NOT AN ENEMY

At my brother's funeral a lady said, "You seem to be doing so well. "

"No, I am doing quite poorly, thank you. " I responded.

She did not give up, and said, "Well, you don't seem to be upset. "

I did not want to get into any discussion, but I had acted like nothing had happened as long as I could, and I reacted.

I said, "If I were doing well with my grief, I would be over in the corner curled up in a fetal position crying, not standing here acting like no one has died. "

We are doing well with our grief when we are grieving. Somehow we have it backwards. We think people are doing well when they aren't crying.

Grief is a process of walking through some painful periods toward learning to cope again. We do not walk this path without pain and tears. When we are in the most pain, we are making the most progress. When the pain is less, we are coasting and resting up for the next steps. People need to grieve. Grief is not an enemy to be avoided; it is a healing path to be walked.

PERMISSION TO GRIEVE

I like to use my soap box to say that we need to allow people to have their grief. Some friends of mine had a child die suddenly and with no explanation. The wife was hysterical, and her husband and the doctor tried to get her to calm down.

She looked at them and said, "Don't take my grief away from me; I deserve it, and I am going to have it."

I have always thought that was the most insightful statement under pressure I have ever heard. I am also glad I was not there. Had I been there, I would have been in the middle of the taking away process. I saw my job as trying to be sure no one grieved—or if they did so they did not grieve in front of me.

I was not comfortable with their pain or their tears. I would do anything to keep from having to deal with people in grief. I thought my job was to cheer everyone up. I would tell jokes at inappropriate times. I would quote scripture. I am sure there are people who would love to cram the King James version down my throat to this day. I thought if I got a family through the funeral without tears, I had done a great job of comforting. I was taking their grief away from them.

We take people's grief away when we try to put the best face on the pain. "Your child died, but it could have been worse; it could have been two children—so cheer up. "

I think we have a set of things we cannot grieve about. Grief is not allowed after a stillborn or a miscarriage. Someone will say, "You can have another child," or "You did not have this one long enough to get attached to it. "

We do not allow women to grieve over a mastectomy. Our attitude usually is,"You are lucky they found it. "Some women do not feel lucky they feel mutilated. One of the most angry women I know is a friend who had a mastectomy, and no one would let her grieve over the loss. She has waited five years for the cancer to return, and has waited the five years in silence.

I was in Washington state to speak at a hospice. The medical director of the hospice had a son who was among the students trapped on Mt. Hood. Eight students were trapped in a snow storm. Six died. The son and an sixteen-year-old girl survived. The day I was there the boy had to have both legs amputated below the knees. I spoke to a city wide forum that night and said, "It will be difficult for us to allow that young man to grieve over the loss of his legs. The tendency will be to tell him how lucky he is to be alive. How could you grieve over your legs? Everyone else died. But he will still miss his legs, won't he?"

It is like the statement, "I felt sorry because I had no shoes until I met a man who had no feet." That statement sounds good but it does not work. In the middle of a West Texas winter I want shoes even if no one has feet.

Grief is a process, and we need to insist that people be given permission and time to walk through the process. Let no one take grief away; rather let us walk though the pain with the grieving person.

GRIEF TAKES TIME

We will give people about three months for their grieving before we decide they are wallowing in their grief. I have no idea where the term "wallowing in grief" originated, but I wish it could be eliminated. The idea is that if we do not pressure people, they will enjoy grieving and never get over it. Grief generally lasts about two years. There is nothing sacred about two years. Some will take longer, and in rare cases some might complete the process in less time. This does not mean folks will hurt all the time for two years. It just means it takes about two years to walk through all of the feelings involved in the death of a loved one.

PEELING THE ONION

This two-year process has some levels most authors call stages. I am not fond of the word "stages." It sounds like clear-cut lines of demarcation. It makes us think that all people walk a set path on a set schedule. Grief is as individual as a fingerprint. We all do grief in our own way and on our on schedule. We cannot box grief into any pattern.

The best definition of grief I know is: "Grief is like peeling an onion; it comes off one layer at a time, and you cry a lot." I like the onion analogy because it allows for the individual differences in grief. If one hundred people were given an onion, no two onions would be alike, and no two people would peel the onions the same way. We do it in our own way.

The onion analogy allows for the differences in the various grieving experiences. Too often we authors make it seem that all grief is the same. Each type of experience has elements that are either different or at least intensified.

A miscarriage, for example, has an element of loneliness about it. The mother is the only one who knows the child. She may have had to guess at the personality, but she does guess and has to explain the significance of a life no one else knows. That is lonely.

A suicide has an element of being shattered. It is as if the onion has been shattered and must be reconstructed before grief can proceed. I am walking with a family whose son committed suicide. They have spent the past year trying to piece together every bit of information, every theory, and every written word in an effort to put the onion back together so the peeling can begin.

The onion analogy pictures the grieving experience. The outside of an onion is a dry hull. This hull can be crumbled into confetti. If we rubbed the hull in our hands until it was crumbled and threw it in the air, it would be a whirl of bits and pieces. That is a picture of the first period of grief. It is a whirl. A thousand questions float around our heads, but none of them land. People in grief ask a question, and before an answer can come they ask another one. Reality comes by and hits for a moment, but does not stay. In the first days after my brother died, the thought that I would never see him again would pass through my mind, but it would be gone before I could grieve. That is the whirl.

Gradually the whirl stops, the questions do not just pass by, and reality comes and sits on the chest. That is the second layer of the onion. This is the reality period of grief. People say their chest hurt; and they do not think they can breath. They call up friends in the middle of the night and cannot remember what they were going to say. This is the time of the most pain. This is the time when they need someone to let them talk. There are no answers to make the pain go away. They could not assimilate an answer if one could be found. They need someone to be there with a listening ear.

Gradually folks move from the reality period to what I call the reaction time. This is when the anger comes. The anger may frighten those who are trying to help, but it is a healthy part of the peeling process. It needs to happen and needs to be allowed. Too often the approach used on anger is to tell folks they should not feel this way. This intensifies the anger. We need to give people the right to feel angry and the right to say they are angry. If people cannot find permission for their anger, the anger can internalize. Internalized anger can come out in illness, substance abuse or guilt. The results can be disastrous.

The last layer of the onion is the reconstruction period. People do decide to live again. I used to call this the recovery period. That sounds like people get well and do not have the problem anymore. They do not get well; they learn to cope in a new way.

People who seem to survive best are the ones who have permission from themselves and others to take the time to peel the onion.

PEOPLE WANT AND NEED TO REMEMBER

There seems to be a universal fear of people remembering those who have died. We must think remembering is somehow unhealthy. More than likely we think like this because of our discomfort in talking about the death. Our discomfort makes us want our friends and loved ones to refrain from talking about the person who has died.

Our concept of grief seems to be designed to forget as soon as possible. I think we clean out closets far too soon. There is no rule for when things should be cleaned out. Everyone must do this in their own way. Some will want to dispose of things almost immediately. Others will make this a part of the grieving process. Everyone should be free to determine their own pace. The problem is that friends and loved ones tend to intrude with advice and help.

It is not unusual for people to barge in and remove the personal belongings while the grieving person is not looking. These are not bad people; they think they are helping. The idea is that an empty closet does not hurt as much as a full one. Seeing the clothes reminds us of the loved one. That hurts, so it is bad. Hurting is not always bad. The presence of hurt means grief is at work, and where grief is allowed to work it brings healing out of the pain.

We are not trying to forget loved ones. We are trying to learn to live with them not being here. We will never forget and should not be asked to do so. Deciding what to do with belongings is part of the process of peeling the onion. Each item becomes symbolic of our walk through grief.

A lady in California told me I had explained her husband's old Packard. It seems he had an old car, and it was one of the loves of his life. When he died everyone told her to sell the car. Their fear was the car would remind her of her husband. She wanted to keep the car for just that reason. She held fast against advice and pressure. She told how much anger she worked off polishing the car. Old Packards had a great deal of chrome, and she would polish it and fuss at her husband for dying. One day she wanted to sell the car. An ad drew an immediate response, and a man bought the car. She said, "When the man drove off in the car, he had the same silly little grin on his face as my husband did the day he bought it, and it was all right."

THE NEEDS

People in pain need what I call the three H'S.
They need us to
    HANG AROUND
        HUG THEM
            AND
                HUSH.

Trust presence. Nothing takes the place of being there. When in doubt—go. There is no substitute for a warm body by our side. We may not know what to say or what not to say. We may not know what to do or what not to do. But if we are there, just there, we are helping.

Trust touch. If a human being needs eight hugs per day to be healthy, then a person in grief may need twice the norm. When the world has turned to sorrow, we need the warmth and security of arms and skin. "Go hug" should be the motto of those who want to comfort.

Trust silence. People who have walked through grief tell me the ones who helped the most were the ones who were just there. They did not impose their ideas or feelings. They were comfortable with silence. I feel so strongly about it that I say, "If you aren't going to hush, then don't go."

SECTION II

THE GIFT OF SIGNIFICANCE

PEOPLE ARE NOT GOING TO MOVE FORWARD
IN THEIR GRIEF UNTIL THE SIGNIFICANCE OF
THE PERSON WHO HAS DIED HAS BEEN EST-
ABLISHED.
PEOPLE WHO CAN ESTABLISH SIGNIFICANCE
MAKE PROGRESS.
THOSE WHO CANNOT DO SO HANG ON AND
HURT.

CHAPTER V

THE GIFT OF SIGNIFICANCE

People often ask me who has the worst kind of grief. It is as if they think they will feel better if they find out their grief is not as bad as someone else's. There may be some who think they will feel better if they find out theirs is worse than anyone else's. I tell them that grief only comes in one size—extra large. There is no way to say which is the worst kind. There is no way to differentiate between the pain. Grief hurts as much as it can hurt.

Most of what I know has come from listening to the stories people tell. Usually the best gifts of insight I have received happened quietly and with no warning. At the time, I often had no idea the story was giving birth to a new concept. In this tradition of learning by listening to stories, I found some great insight from a woman from Missouri.

This woman's husband had died after a brief marriage. Later she remarried, and then one of her children died. She found the words to describe the differences in these two experiences.

She said, "I do not think I can differentiate between the pain. In both experiences it hurts so much you almost go blind. The difference is in the grieving process. The grief after the death of a mate is a process of turning loose—of saying goodbye. The grief following the death of a child is a process of hanging on—of refusing to say goodbye.

The difference is the mate has had the chance to establish identity and significance. The child has not lived long enough to complete these tasks. The parent is left feeling they must establish significance for the child. It is almost as if you must "walk through the world for the child." After I had the chance to think through the differences, I realized two very important insights.

The first insight is that anyone who experiences the death of a child will almost kiss the person who is willing to talk about the child. One aspect of establishing significance is being sure the child is not forgotten. They want the child remembered. They long to hear the child's name. They are hungry for the chance to talk about the child with someone who is comfortable with the conversation.

We are reluctant to call the child's name for fear of reminding the parents (as if they have forgotten) or for fear of opening up old wounds (as if they are healed over).

The second insight concerns a new understanding of the grief process. In both the death of a mate and the death of a child the key word was significance. She could say goodbye to a mate because significance was there. She could not say goodbye to the child because significance was not established. I think that mother's story gives us a clue to helping people walk through the grieving process. I had never seen the connection before, but now I see tremendous implications.

People are not going to move forward in their grief until the significance of the person has been established. People who can establish significance will move forward. Those who cannot will hang on and hurt.

There are two schedules in grief or pain. The first schedule is when the pain starts, and the second is when the person gets ready to do something about the pain. Often there is a great span of time between these schedules. The presence of hurt does not mean the person is ready to deal with the hurt. Waiting for people to get ready to do something about their pain is one of the hardest things a caregiver has to face. We watch folks hurt and suffer while our hands are tied until they get ready. We know they will hurt until they are ready to let go and begin to move through the grief, but we also know that people move when they are ready—not when we think they should be ready. The watching and waiting is difficult.

I think the wait relates to significance. In my experience it has been the ones who have not found a way to establish significance that have waited the longest before getting ready to move into the grief process. It has also been my experience that some who are unable to establish significance never move at all.

MEMORIES AND SIGNIFICANCE

The grieving process is a gradual change from the physical presence of a loved on to the sense of presence provided by the memories. The goal is to learn to live with the person not being here. Coping without presence happens when we begin to find comfort in the memories. It is difficult to move into memories if we are still in need of proving the value of the person who has died. The need to prove can lock us into the past. This may be the key to some people becoming blocked in the grieving process.

I am often asked if people get stuck in the grieving process, and if they do, what can be done to help them begin to move again. People do get stuck. There are not as many stuck as most people think, because we tend to decide they are stuck after about three months. I do not consider anyone to be stuck until two years have passed. We need to give plenty of time before we decide they are stuck.

Stuck people will go over the same ground again and again. Nothing we say will have any effect. Every solution we give is met with an immediate rejection and a list of reasons why the suggestion will not work. This behavior says the person does not want to get well.

When I am called upon to deal with a person in this condition, I ask them what they are getting out of their grieving. They always protest and say they are getting nothing at all. I gently suggest they are getting something or they would not be there. Hopefully I can get them to move off of high-center and continue progressing again.

The better answer is to help people move through the grieving process without getting stuck. Prevention is much preferred to cure. The ones most likely to become stuck in the process are the ones who cannot move from presence to memories. Somehow they cannot stand to turn loose of the presence and begin to cope with the absence. Memories do not interest them; they want it back like it was. They want that or nothing. They live for denial.

One of the best things we can do to keep people from

becoming stuck is to help them establish significance. The first thing I talk about after a death is the value of the person who died. On the surface this seems to be counterproductive. We seem to be making the loss greater instead of lessening the load. It seems to be the wrong way, but it works wonders. The more we are willing to let them talk about the person, and the more they can tell what the person means to them the sooner they can establish significance and move on. The pattern is establish first and move second.

Time has a hard time healing if significance is not established. I have a friend who leads grief recovery groups for a funeral home. He decided to lead a group on stillborns and miscarriages. The first night of the group there was an elderly woman waiting for him when he arrived. When my friend asked her if he could help, she was hesitant to say she had come to attend the stillborn group. He assured her she was welcome, and she began to tell him her story.

"Fifty years ago I had a stillborn son. Fifty years ago when a child was stillborn, the husband would take the child out for burial. Often the mother was never even told where the child was buried. The idea was that we would not grieve if we did not have to face the loss. My husband took our son out for burial, and when he returned he told me the child was in the past and we must move on. I was to never talk about the child," she said.

"For fifty years I have obeyed my husband and the other members of my family. I have never talked about my son. I have watched other boys grow to manhood and wondered what my son would look like or be like. My husband is dead now, and I want to talk," she continued.

"The first thing I want to say is, I named him Tommy. No one knows he even has a name. I have never told a soul, but I want it known that I have a son named Tommy."

My friend is a Catholic deacon, and with great insight and compassion he led this lady in a prayer service for Tommy. She was given the gift of closure and found the gift of significance fifty years late.

THE SEARCH FOR SIGNIFICANCE

Grief ignored does not go away. Significance not found does not work itself out. The first effort a family will make is the effort to show how significant the person was. I called a friend whose fifteen-year-old son had died suddenly. The first two things he said were, "Andrew was a wonderful child, a real joy, and the church was packed for his funeral." He was telling the story of significance.

Often the search for significance is camouflaged behind the questions and reactions of grieving. Usually the first question a person asks is, "Why did this happen to me?" That is the natural and honest response we would expect. Usually we try to explain the reasons as best we can. Underneath this question they are asking, "Was this person not important enough to live? Did they matter?"

The second question is, "Will I survive?" They are expressing a normal response to the pain, of course, but they are also trying to verbalize the depth of their loss. That is another way of expressing the significance of the person who has died.

When they wonder about God and whether this happened as a punishment for their wrongs, they can also be saying, "This person was so meaningful there must be a profound reason for their death. This cannot be just happenstance."

The first need is for the family to think through how

significant the person was to them. I have loved a wife for many years, but I do not really know how much she means to me. There are so many things I take for granted. She has meaning to me that I have not realized. If she dies I will need time to reevaluate her worth and place in my life. When a family member starts this process it can seem like they are not being rational. We tend to think they are deifying the person who has died. If we are not careful we will tend to try to make them see the person in a "realistic light". The problem is that our efforts tend to take away a needed period of coming to grips with the depth of the loss. The depth must be explored fully before the loss can be adequately dealt with.

There is a need to establish significance even if the relationship was not the best. No relationship is all good, and none is all bad. The good needs to be appreciated. The bad needs to be acknowledged with honesty and candor.

A lady told me of her ambivalent feelings after the death of her husband. Their thirty year marriage was marred by the husband's lack of feelings. After his death she told me she did not know what to feel. On the one hand there was a feeling of relief that the bad part was over. On the other hand she was beginning to see how much the rest of the relationship meant to her, and was feeling genuine sorrow over the loss of that part of the marriage. She felt the need to let herself feel the loss, and the need to tell others how much her husband meant to her, but she thought she was being hypocritical if she expressed these feelings while she felt a sense of relief at the same time. She was also afraid all of her friends who knew the truth about the marriage would not understand her new appreciation of her husband.

Establishing significance involves this kind of honest

reevaluation of the meaning of the person who has died. She was not being a hypocrite. She was simply doing the necessary, and healing, work of significance.

The second phase of establishing significance is the need to be sure those outside the family thought the person was significant. This creates a ready made conflict. Most of the friends will be trying to help the person forget and move on, while the person needs desperately to hear that the friends remember and miss the person who has died.

This is why we need to take great care in our comfort.

CAREFUL COMFORT

I hesitate to say anything critical about the way we comfort. The last thing I want to do is scare people about what to say to hurting people. Most of us are already so frightened that we avoid talking to every hurting person possible. Our fear of saying the wrong things leaves many grievers with no one to talk to or cry with at all.

Hesitantly, then I need to carefully state that often our efforts at making folks feel better makes it harder for them to establish significance. When we try to dismiss the loss as a blessing we can leave the impression, however unintended, that the person did not matter.

When we tell a mother of a stillborn that they can have another child, or that she did not have that one long enough to get attached, we are saying this child did not matter (is not significant).

When we explain away the death by saying the person is better off, the grieving person may hear us say that the life here was not of value or importance.

When we say, "God will not put more on us than we can bear," we are saying, "This loss is not an unbearable burden." In the process we trivialize the loss. I hear more anger at this statement than any of the others people usually use. The anger is directed at the trivialization, not at the statement.

Great care should be taken in trying to comfort by explanation. Our best efforts can come across as trivializing. A ministers wife gushed to a friend of mine whose husband had died four months earlier, "I know you must be hurting during this Christmas season, but isn't it a great comfort knowing that Carl is spending his first Christmas with the Lord."

My friend said, "No it is no comfort at all. He should be spending it with me."

It seems to be the opposite of what will help people, but we need to understand and relate to the loss as a loss. "Your husband died, and I know you must be devastated. A huge chunk has been bitten out of your heart, and it will not grow back. You will learn to live again, but the chunk will never grow back." These statements seem to add to the loss and pain, but the effect is that we acknowledge and underscore the significance of the person and the loss rather than trivializing the life and the loss.

Somehow we have become convinced that sympathy makes people worse. "If we sympathize, they will just wallow in pity and never get well." Sympathy is not harmful. Sympathy is understanding the feelings of those in pain. Sympathy is empathy into that pain. Sympathy says the person has a right to hurt and they do not need to play down the pain nor the anger attached to that hurt. Sympathy is careful comfort.

CHAPTER VI

BUILDING SIGNIFICANCE
THE ROLE OF THE FUNERAL

One of the joys of being an author is the phone calls I receive from people I do not know. Recently a lady called early one Saturday morning. We had talked a few weeks earlier about her husband being terminal. Now she called to tell me of his death. As soon as she told me he had died, she began telling me about the service: the number of people who attended, the flowers that covered the front of the church, and the beauty of the music. She saw the funeral as her gift of love to her husband. She said, "To show you what a good person he was, I have received over one hundred and fifty cards." Then she told me she had mailed me the newspaper write-ups about her husband. This lady was building significance, and it began with the funeral.

The funeral has been kicked around and criticized until I am almost afraid to say anything good about it. I have heard all of the arguments about how "plastic" funerals are, and how our practice of memorializing the dead is pagan.

The current trend away from funerals is a concern to me. We need to enhance the funeral experience, not do away with the whole process. An ever growing number of people are opting for just a brief service at the grave side. An even larger percentage are trying to have nice little antiseptic services that never mention death or loss. There seems to be a trend toward making the funeral a production for the entertainment of the audience instead of a time for discovering the significance of the person.

At a recent service the son of the man who died insisted on shoveling the dirt into the grave. He was very nice about it and organized it so it did not interfere in any way. After the people left, he and certain close friends lovingly covered the casket of his father. That sounds like a throwback to the dark ages, but the son found great meaning in this loving act. Family participation may well be the key we have been looking for in making the funeral a healing experience. Somehow the idea of the family taking part and facing the death sounds much more healing to me than to gather for a service and act as if no one died.

There are some things about the funeral I would change of course, but there is much about the funeral that is healthy and healing. When the funeral offers the family the time to reflect on the life lived among them, then the funeral is healthy. When the presence of friends conveys the importance of the loved one to the family, then the funeral is healthy. I think the presence of flowers is important. The current trend is to request donations to some charity in lieu of flowers, but the flowers say this person is significant. The key is whatever gives significance gives health.

When the spoken words help the family face the loss instead of denying the existence of death, then the funeral is healthy. The funeral can be the first step in establishing significance. If we lose the funeral we will lose one of the most helpful steps in the healing process.

This may produce a problem for some of the clergy. I come from the tradition of preaching to the living and avoiding any glorification of the person who died. I have had to struggle to see the value of sharing the meaning of the life instead of preaching a sermon. Other clergy persons will have come from the tradition of the service being one of worshiping God through certain rituals and sacraments. Seeing the funeral in any other light is not easy.

Although much of it is undeserved, the clergy receive more criticism about the funeral and the counseling of the grieving family than they do regarding any other area. The criticism I hear the most is that we do not personalize the funeral. We are accused of having a set sermon that we use for every funeral. I hear how we do not even call the person's name. It seems to me that one of the answers to the criticism is to personalize the funeral as much as our tradition and beliefs will allow.

I hope there is a future for the funeral. I hope that future produces new ways to present the value of the person. We are beginning to see some new ideas being tried. I recently saw a video that had been prepared about a young mother who had died. The video was tastefully done and seemed to be a natural part of the service.

These new ideas may be part of the answer for the clergy. Many of these could be done by the funeral directors. This would personalize the service and still allow the clergy to function within his or her convictions.

I hope funeral directors will take a more active part in the service. Maybe they can act as master of ceremonies. Every clergy person is called on to direct funerals for people we do not know and who do not know us. Often we have no time to meet with the family much less find any information to help personalize. It would be a great help to have the funeral director assist in this part of the service.

It would be a further help to have someone direct the service and make introductions. I do not enjoy getting up before an audience that has no idea who I am or why I am there.

I am convinced that somehow we must continue the search for methods to make the funeral have a key and vital role in a healthy approach to death.

THE ROLE OF THE FUTURE

At a conference on Long Island, New York, a person talked about her lifelong search for her roots. Her family migrated from Europe during the beginning of World War II. The town of her roots was destroyed, and all records burned. She told how incomplete she felt until she made a trip to the town. Here she found some records were intact, and she could find the graves of some of her kinsmen. I had very little appreciation for the location of graves until I heard her story and the stories that followed her telling. Since that time I tell her story, and I am amazed at what the telling of it generates in others.

These stories give me a different perspective on the connection we have with the past. I think the burial place has meaning we may have missed. This means we should be careful about scattering the ashes of loved ones. It sounds wonderful and dramatic to have ashes scattered from some mountain or thrown from an airplane, but future generations may need a place where that person is buried. There is something about having a place.

I am going to make a pilgrimage to North Carolina for the express purpose of standing where my roots are buried. It will have meaning. Having a place seems to be important to me. I seem to feel connected to my past and somehow fit into the scheme of things because of this tangible evidence of my roots.

STARTING THE MEMORIES

Significance must be established, it cannot be imagined. No matter what the format, the family needs time to discover and discuss the value of the person. This further strengthens my resolve that the family needs to view the body of the one who has died. A time together in that setting somehow begins the process of reality and closure. It also begins the process of memories and significance.

The night before my grandmother's funeral my Father said, "Let's go down to the funeral home and visit with Momma Hoyle." We sat around her casket and told Momma Hoyle stories for an hour or two. I do not remember anything that was said during the funeral, but I will remember that night for the rest of my life. We began the story telling process that night, and it has continued. She died in 1955, Her body was dead, but she is as alive in our family now as she was in my youth.

Since that night I gather the immediate family of the person who has died together the night before a funeral, and we have a time of remembering together. Often the men in the family are reluctant to come. They are afraid the session will get intimate or, as they call it, "morbid." Not one of these sessions has ever become morbid. Most of the sessions are times of telling funny stories. I watch the younger generations at these sessions. It is wonderful for them to see the significance of the person develop before their eyes.

I did these sessions for years before I discovered the value of the stories. Families who deny at the funeral home tend to deny at home. Often the family will act as if nothing has happened. Family members tend not to want to talk about the pain they feel until they know how much pain the other person is feeling. Both sides end up waiting and avoiding the subject. This involves the fear of intimacy. Most of us are afraid to tap into areas of deep feeling for fear we will get in over our heads.

When my wife's father died, Barbara and I both went on as if nothing had happened. After a period of a few weeks I finally could not stand it, and started talking about how I missed him and what he meant. We broke through the barrier and began to grieve together.

This time for the family breaks through these barriers and starts the family sharing their pain and telling the stories that give significance.

NOURISH THE MEMORIES

The modern day approach to grief seems to be an effort to forget. Significance is an effort to remember. Significance needs to be nourished. Significance is based on stories. Life stories told over and over by the ones the person touched. Nothing feels better to a family than the thought that the person will be remembered and have stories told about their life. Somehow that keeps them alive in us.

I love characters. I have collected characters most of my life. I can spend hours telling the stories of these colorful people who touched my life. I come from a family of characters. My family has a tradition of telling the stories at every opportunity. We have heard the stories so often that I not only know what stories will be told, I know the order in which they will be told.

The story telling keeps the person alive. Because of these stories my children know family members who died before I was born. I could draw a picture of Uncle Johnson. I know he was a rather fat man who wore his shoes laced with bailing wire and sat on the front porch every Sunday afternoon and entertained all who would gather to hear his stories. His forte was to make fun of himself and his children. He was a delightful man. He died when I was three years old. I know him through the stories.

LIFE STORIES

One great way to establish significance for ourselves as well as future generations is by recording or writing life stories. One of my hobbies is recording life stories. I tape record up to five hours of the life of elderly people. I have a wonderful time in the process and develop a new appreciation of the history of my area. Future generations will know the stories that tell about lives and people of another time. These tapes are treasured now, and time will increase their worth.

I tried to get my brother to write up his war stories before he died. He told some of the most wonderful and funny stories I have ever heard. I am afraid these stories will be lost to the family. Unfortunately his illness was too fast and sapped too much energy for him to record or write. I have pledged myself to writing the stories for him. I want to preserve them for his grandchildren to enjoy. I have a feeling the greatest good from the writing will be the good it does for me to establish and record the significance of a person I loved.

Stated briefly, significance means: No one is dead until they are forgotten.

SECTION III

THE GIFT OF UNDERSTANDING

WHEN THE PSYCHOLOGIST FINISHES THE
ANALYSIS AND THE COUNSELOR COMPLETES
THE PROBE, WHEN FRIENDS HAVE GIVEN ALL
THE ADVICE THEY KNOW,
AND MATES HAVE TOLD AND RE-TOLD,
THE BOTTOM LINE REMAINS THE SAME.
BASICALLY, WE JUST WANT TO BE UNDERSTOOD.

CHAPTER VII

UNDERSTOOD

Significance and **Understanding** are the two great words used in this book. The longer I live, the more I realize that most of us just want to be understood. "I understand how you feel," may be the sweetest words in our language. These words are only sweet when the understanding is real. If someone says they know just how we feel, when it is evident they have no idea, then the words make us angry. But when the words come from someone who has listened to us and tuned into our feelings then there are no words more affirming. I understand means someone accepts and understands what we think and feel. Being understood makes our thoughts and feelings become legitimate.

After years as a marriage counselor, I think the bottom line in marriage is the search for someone who will understand and accept us. If a woman comes into my office with a list of complaints she has gathered over a long period of time, I begin to look for the reasons behind the list. Most of the time she has never felt her thoughts and feelings have been understood. The lack of understanding creates the anger that forms the list of complaints.

It feels good when we say something stupid and no one tells us how stupid it was.

We feel important when we say something wrong and no one jumps on us or corrects us.

It is wonderful to be out of touch with reality and not have someone call us crazy.

All of that is contained in the wonderful statement, "I understand."

In grief the real healing friends are the ones who understand how we feel. They do not try to fix it. They do not try to put a better face on it. They do not try to explain it away. All of these are efforts at comfort, but they end up trivializing our feelings. Trivializing infuriates people.

The need to be understood is the reason the self-help groups and organizations provide a high level of healing. Helping people find a group may be the best help we can give. Finding a group of people who are walking the same path, feeling the same pain, and able to understand can give great comfort. There is no need to explain. There is no need to be embarrassed when tears come at the worst possible moment. The people in the group understand, and the understanding allows the person in pain to relax. Relaxation does not happen until there is understanding.

I titled one of my books DON'T TAKE MY GRIEF AWAY FROM ME.

The title really says: don't try to explain it away; just understand and walk with folks. The bottom line in helping people walk through grief is empathy for how they feel. We try to understand how they feel instead of telling them how we think they should feel. The bottom line in the search for significance is that the person in grief wants us to relate to the depth of their loss. That is another way of saying they want us to understand.

THE MOST POWERFUL PART
OF THE HUMAN BODY

Understanding requires us to learn how to use the most powerful part of the human body. I think the most powerful organ we have is the ear. Some people would say the brain or the tongue is the most powerful, but I think the ear wins hands down. I even think I can prove my point.

All of us have been angry. I mean really angry... stew for three days kind of angry. We finally told someone about the anger, and while we were telling them we began to notice we were not feeling the same intensity. We could not make the incident seem as bad as it was when it happened. We finally said something like, "Well, you had to be there." While we were talking listening ears were bleeding off the anger. That is the power of the ear.

Psychologists have told us for years that we need to get our anger out—to express how we feel. I think psychology has missed it. It takes two to deal with anger. It takes someone to say how they feel, and it takes someone to hear it. It does no good to express it unless there is someone to hear it.

The listening ear has wonderful powers to help work

through depression, fear, and of course the pain of grief.

I even told a famous television evangelist that I was a divine healer. He was not overly impressed, but I told him the difference between us was that he wanted to lay hands on people and I wanted to lay ears on them. I think ears work best.

The listening ear gives insight. People find insight into their problems and pains when they are listened to much more readily than when they are told. As we lay ears on them, they begin to understand themselves and work through the pain.

Listening heals. People talk grief to death. They will wear out several sets of ears in the process of walking through grief. Often we feel inadequate and do not know what to say to people in pain. It helps to remember that when we listen we are healing. We do not have to say anything. I saw an example of this at a memorial in Washington D.C.

I went to the Viet Nam Memorial. I do not know of any other place that has the same aura as this memorial. I cannot walk down the wall without crying, and I do not know anyone whose name is on the wall. There is something about that black marble wall, with the names of every person who died in the war engraved in chronological order according to when they died, that stirs deep feelings in me and most everyone who visits.

I walked by one of the guides whose job it is to help people locate names on the wall. A veteran of Viet Nam had this guide by the elbow and would not let go. He was telling the guide about his experiences in the war. As I walked by I heard him tell about how they defoliated the trees. I missed the meaning of this encounter. All I could think of was how the guide must feel having his work interrupted. After I left the park I realized that I should have relieved that guide. The veteran did not care who he told, he just needed to tell his story, and he needed to tell it right there. If I lived in Washington D.C., I hope I would have the sensitivity to go spend time at the wall listening to veterans tell their stories. That is healing.

I often speak to a group called The Compassionate Friends. These are people who have suffered the death of a child. My speeches may not help these people very much at all. If I help them it is after the speech. I find a place to sit and sometimes stay two hours after the meeting while these folks line up for a chance to tell their story. They want to talk about their child.

At many of the group meetings the participants bring pictures of their children and place them on a bulletin board. To an outsider that may seem morbid. To these people it is a chance to tell the story.

I spoke for this group at one of their national conventions. They had a large bulletin board full of pictures. Every time I had a break I would go to the board. I would not be there a minute before someone would begin to show me a picture and tell me their story.

At one of their regional meetings I was asked to be interviewed for the newspaper. When I entered the room, the reporter was crying. I asked her what was the matter. She said, "I did not want to come out here. I knew it would be morbid. I have dreaded it for weeks. The first thing I saw when I came in was those pictures."

I said, "Those pictures are not morbid. These people want to tell their stories, and it is important enough that they will put up pictures in order to get the chance to tell it one more time."

People want to be understood, which is another way of saying they want to be heard more than they want to be told.

Walking people through a loss means we need to hear and understand several aspects of the grieving process. Many times these aspects will be missed or misunderstood by almost everyone else. If we can listen and understand, we can heal.

UNDERSTAND ANGER

The least understood aspect of grief is the presence of anger. It always seems to come as a surprise, both to the griever and to those of us who are trying to help. There is anger in grief, and it is healthy. The anger motivates people through the process. The grieving person hits bottom, gets mad, and decides to fight back. This fighting back decision pushes them to peel the next layer of the onion.

The problem with anger is that it needs a place to focus. It is not enough to be angry; we need to be angry at something or someone.

Anger may focus irrationally. It is common for a widow to get angry at her husband for dying. Since this is usually an irrational focus, we assume it is bad for people. It is actually a good place for the anger to focus, as long as the widow can understand that her feelings are normal and she is not crazy.

Often the anger focuses on the clergy. I have been amazed at how often this happens. When I was in the ministry, I had no idea how much criticism I was receiving in this area. The minister is in a vulnerable position. So much is expected of the clergy. Much more is expected than can be delivered. A clergy person cannot be the grief counselor for the congregation. He or she may want to do so, but there are not that many hours in the day. It is physically impossible. When the clergy cannot meet the expectations, the result can be anger. Most of the anger after grief is caused by the fact that anger must focus somewhere, and the clergy person is available.

The tragedy is the ones we help the most are often the ones who become the harshest critics. This can be a heartbreaking experience for the clergy person. I have stood with men and women of the clergy and seen them shake their heads in wonder while they say, "What more could I have done?" Often there is not anything more that could have been done.

I think clergy persons need to protect themselves by teaching their people about grief and the anger involved so the rest of the parish will understand.

Sometimes the anger focuses on God. This causes a certain amount of discomfort and fear among the friends of the grieving person. They are afraid the person will never get over the anger at God. Most of the people who get mad at God and do not get over it are the ones who were attacked for feeling that way about God. If I find someone who is angry with God, I quote a nursery rhyme to myself. The rhyme is: Leave them alone... they will come home, wagging their tails behind them. If we leave them alone, they will come home.

Physicians, funeral directors, family members and mates can be targets of anger's focus. All of these targets make us uncomfortable and may create problems for us, but they are not unhealthy places for anger to focus.

The one place we do not want anger to focus is inward. We do not want the person to focus the anger on themselves. I am amazed at how often the anger turns inward. We can know when it has done so because the person will begin to obsessively play the game of "if-only." Notice I said obsessively: everyone in grief will play some if-only. Internalized anger plays the game obsessively. They will build elaborate scenarios proving the death was somehow their fault. Sometimes what seems to be guilt in grief is actually anger internalized.

A lady whose daughter-in-law was murdered said, "I went with the kids when they were looking for an apartment. I found that apartment house. I took them to see it and suggested that they consider living there. Now if I had not found that apartment, they would not have been in that apartment. If they were not in that apartment, the person would not have found her there, and she would still be alive, so it is my fault."

On the surface it seems this lady is feeling guilt. Underneath the surface is anger that has nowhere to go, so it is internalizing. That is the kind of anger that does damage. That kind of anger needs to re-focus.

RE-FOCUSING ANGER

We do not re-focus anger by trying to re-focus anger. That sounds like a paradox, but we do not get people to stop being angry by telling them they should not feel the way they feel. We re-focus anger by helping them discover that anger is what they are feeling. When they discover that anger is what they are feeling, they will quite often re-focus the anger themselves. If we try to tell them how to feel, they will resist, and the resistance will intensify the anger.

I rode in a car for several hours with a couple whose daughter had committed suicide. For the first hour of the trip they could talk of nothing except how their pastor and church had failed them in their time of need. After a time the talking began to show signs of having bled off some of the anger. I said, "May I tell you what I

69

am hearing you say?" They gave permission and I said, "I am hearing you say you are angry. It is alright to be angry. You should be angry."

I am no miracle worker but in thirty minutes their anger had re-focused. I followed them for two years, and the anger never again focused on the church or the pastor. Just before we reached our destination the wife said, "You know why I have been so angry at my friends?" I said "No, why?" She said, "Because I do not want to be angry at my daughter."

Anger is re-focused by the bleeding—off process of being heard and understood. Instructions and arguments may only intensify it.

UNDERSTAND THE NEED TO BE NORMAL

If I have a calling in life, it is to prove to people how normal they are. Most of us do not think we are normal. We think we have thoughts and feelings no one else has, at least no one in their right mind. The longer I live the more I believe that we are all very much alike. The problem is we have no way of knowing how other people think or feel. No one tells us the whole story, so we must guess. Most of the time our guessing makes us feel odd.

I have had problems with church because of this never telling the whole story. In church all we hear are the successes. We never hear the failures. Usually someone gets up and says something like, "I was having trouble with my car, and I prayed about it, and God gave me a new Oldsmobile and an airplane." No one ever gets up and says, "I was having trouble with my car and I prayed about it, and the motor fell out of the thing." That also happens, but we never hear about it.

In caring for loved ones through illness we only hear

one side of the story. We hear the reports of how someone stood by and loved a person through the illness until they died. The story is always warm and full of blessings. It is always a wonderful experience. No one tells the other side. No one tells how tired we get. No one tells how angry we get. No one says that by the time death comes, we often are ready for it to be over.

Many of the people we deal with in grief are struggling with feelings they had during the family member's illness... feelings they think no one else ever felt... feelings they think mean they did not love properly.

My father decided to die on July 5, 1985. It took him eight months to complete his mission. During those months I tried to arrange my schedule to be with him and care for his needs. That was tough because I make my living speaking all over the country.

No one told me how tiring that can become. No one told me how it feels to get home past midnight dead tired, only to need to go to one's father's side for another time of crisis. No one told me how to react when I put him in the bathtub, and he promptly messed in the water. No one told me that I would want to pull the stopper on the tub and let him go down the drain.

No one told me that I would want it to be over. That means I was ready for my father to die. I wanted it to be over because he was in a race with pain, and I wanted him to win. I also wanted it to be over because I was tired and needed some relief. These feelings are normal.

After a death someone needs to hear and understand the pent up feelings people are afraid to share because they think the feelings prove they are crazy or did not love like they should. These feelings come out when we hear, understand, and begin to share our own feelings with openness and honesty.

If the feelings do not come out the person is a most likely candidate for overcompensation. Since they cannot feel as they think they should, they will try to make sure everyone else feels good about the person who died. These are the ones who almost deify the person who died. These are the ones who seem to get stuck in the grieving process and never move. These people need to be heard and understood.

UNDERSTANDING THE ROLE CHANGES

Anytime we experience a change in our roles, we will experience a time when it is difficult to communicate.

The role changed between my father and me, and I became the parent. When this happened, our communication went from relaxed and intimate to strained and formal. I was uncomfortable when he was around and had very little to say. I thought I had stopped loving my father. When I confronted the issue, I found out he was also uncomfortable around me and could not understand how the relationship could turn so suddenly.

Any role change has an effect on communication. I often joke about my children going to bed as angelic twelve-year-old girls and waking up the next morning as thirteen-year- old demons. Communication was almost impossible for several months.

When a death occurs, the family must go through some rather drastic role changes. Nothing is the same. Suddenly each family member must redefine their role and standing in the family.

Children can become parents to parents. Parents can feel resentment over being replaced and dependent. One child can be chosen as the one responsible for the remaining parent with the other children acting as critics on the performance.

Siblings suddenly find their roles undefined. Sisters who have been best friends for most of their lives can find themselves squabbling over possessions they do not even want. Family members tend to team up against each other, and the entire extended family can be polarized. They can have disagreements during this time that last for years.

Families need to understand that these feelings are normal. They are not the only ones to have a squabble at the funeral of a loved one. They are not the only ones to go through a time of redefining roles.

They need to understand that the things said or done during this time are the result of the redefining and tension. Everything should be judged from the perspective of this tension and redefinition. If families can understand the what is happening during this period, they have a better chance at forgiveness and restoration.

The family needs to understand that this period will pass. As new roles are established the need for struggle and taking sides will diminish, and they can become family again. The understanding must come from someone who sees through the situation and is available to listen and lead the family.

Often I broach the subject, even if there is no evident indication that tension exists between the family members. I simply begin talking about the role changes I have experienced and the fact that role changes produce a need to restructure communications. Most of the time that leads to a discussion that helps them understand the tensions, and perhaps squabbles, they are experiencing. Once again understanding heals.

UNDERSTAND DEPRESSION

A couple whose son had accidentally hanged himself came to one of my seminars. We had dinner together and then visited late into the night. All through our time together the woman kept saying, "I just don't want to go on."

When someone says they do not want to go on, the first thing we think of is suicide. Are they thinking about killing themselves? When I asked her about suicide, she said there was no way she would do that to her family. The next logical step is to tell her all the reasons she has for going on. When I suggested the reasons she said, "I know I should go on—I know I am going to go on. The problem is I don't want to."

Suddenly it was clear. There is a form of depression that causes a lack of feelings rather than the normal blue feelings we usually expect with depression. This form of depression is often present in the grief process.

The lack of feelings can be frightening. People wonder if they are ready to give up on life, or if the lack of feelings means they did not love. Lack of feelings has the most profound effect on women. Women are more attuned to feelings than most men and are more dependent on feelings to motivate and sustain them. When a woman cannot feel, she does not think she can function.

The lady was trying to say that she knew she was going on, but she thought there should be a desire to do so. She felt emotionally flat and wondered if this meant she did not love her husband and the remaining child. She did not know how to function without wanting to do so. All of her life her feelings had been there to motivate and guide, now she was flat and felt detached and lost.

As we talked I began to understand what she was saying. Just finding someone who understood and did not tell her how or why she should feel did her a world of good. We talked together about depression. I could promise her that the feelings would return. In time the depression would lift, and feelings that are still there but are choked off will re-surface. The feelings would return much sooner if she could accept the lack of feelings as normal and stop fighting herself. Her fighting herself creates more tension and fear, and buries the feelings even deeper.

I told her that until the feelings returned, it was a matter of putting one foot in front of the other, and that it was alright to not feel anything and just put one foot in front of the other. Many people we deal with are in this kind of depression. They need to be understood and know they are normal. Once again we just lay ears on them.

CHAPTER VIII

KEYS TO CARING

I hope this book has made it easier to help people in pain. I think there is a danger of making grief so mysterious no one will dare try to help people ever again. Helping is a simple process of listening until we understand. I think there are three keys to becoming a caregiver to those in grief. They are simple words with great impact.

FOCUS

I sat with a mother whose son had hanged himself about three weeks earlier. We met for lunch and spent three hours talking through some of her pain. The next time we got together she said something that I took as a compliment, and then saw it in a much deeper way.

She said, "When I got home, I realized that you had

listened to me for three hours. I am forty-three years old, and that is the first time in my life anyone ever listened just to me for three hours."

After the compliment wore off, it hit me that most of the people in the world would have to say the same thing this lady said: "No one has ever listened to me for three hours." That takes focus, but it works. Focus means we hear what is being said. Focus means we notice everything possible about people. Focus means we concentrate on the person instead of trying to figure out what we are going to say when it is our turn to talk. Focus is understanding.

COMFORT

Comfort is the most difficult key. It is hard to get comfortable with listening. It is hard to get comfortable with the emotion and intimacy of grief. It is even harder to get comfortable with just listening when people are in pain. We think we have not done anything until we have said something. In grief there is nothing to say that will make the pain go away.

As we mentioned in a previous chapter, people in grief need three H's. They need us to hang around—-hug them—-and hush. It is hard to hush.

People in grief usually lose friends in addition to losing the one who has died. This happens most often because the friends cannot get comfortable just listening. They think they must say something and can't think of anything to say. This leads to discomfort and can ultimately lead to rejection.

I have a friend whose son was killed in a plane crash. Before the accident there were four couples in his group. They were so thick they whipped each other's children. Today, if any of the other couples see him coming they will cross the street to avoid him. If any of them was asked what happened, they would say, "He just wallowed in his grief." The truth is they went over there the night it happened and could not figure out what to say. After a time of agony and discomfort they left, saying, "We will go now, but if there is anything we can do just let us know."

The experience was so uncomfortable they dreaded going back. The dread led to delay. The delay led to guilt. Then they had to get angry with the man to justify their guilt. The result is the man lost a son and six friends at the same time.

I think a great deal of the tension caregivers feel comes from a lack of comfort with or belief in the power of listening. We tend to go home at night and rehash the day, trying to figure out what we should have said.

I cannot name the number of people who feel terrible guilt because they have forsaken friends in need. They did not go because they felt uncomfortable. They felt uncomfortable because they did not know what to say.

We need to understand that there are no verbal salves that will make the pain go away. People get insight when they talk and we listen. In time we can get proficient in the skill of listening. Much later we can even get comfortable with our silence.

TIMING

It is not what we say nor how we say it; it is when we say it that makes the difference. We can say anything we want to and not be offensive, after they know we have heard them. Anything we say before they know we have heard them can be offensive.

There is a place for our insight, but it is after we have heard them.

There is a place for scripture, but it is after we have heard them. If we stand at the door and throw Bible verses at them they will throw them back almost every time.

There is a place for prayer, but it is after we have heard them.

General George Marshal created a three step formula for dealing with conflict.

Step one: Let the other person tell their story.

Step Two: Let the other person tell their whole story.

Step Three: Let the other person tell their whole story first.

What works in conflict works even better in caregiving. Let them tell their whole story first.

SECTION IV

THE GIFT OF PERSONAL CARE

AFTER ALL OF THE BOOKS HAVE BEEN READ.
THE SEMINARS EXPERIENCED,
AND THE SPEECHES HEARD,
SOMEONE MUST REACH OUT AND TOUCH.

CHAPTER IX

CARING IS MAKING SURE

I thought this book was finished until I realized there is a need for some ideas on how to give practical and personal care. Sometimes I think we authors get so caught up in our concepts about how the grieving process works that we forget most people want to help, but do not know how.

Most of the help people receive will come from their friends. Unfortunately, most of the hurt they will receive will also come from their friends. If the friends are going to help, they must find practical and personal ways to touch.

Matter of fact, the professionals among us need to find practical and personal ways to touch. We can become wonderful theoreticians and lead marvelous seminars and still not touch.

I read about a person who all of his life wanted to be a fireman. He dreamed of fighting fires. When he graduated from college he was asked to study abroad. When he finished his studies, he went on to a great career as a teacher and consultant in fire fighting. He became known all over the world. On his death bed he said, "All I ever wanted to do was fight fires. I have never gotten to fight a real fire. Not one real fire."

I have met some people who have found their own personal ways to give care. I think caring is making sure. It is finding the little things that others miss, and being sure they are provided for or looked after. Each of these people has found a way to make sure something is done. In each case the something is important. In each case the something is not as important as the person doing the something.

I think the best way to allow these people to inspire us to find our own something is to simply tell their stories.

THE ONE WHO CLEANS BATHROOMS

I met a very dignified lady as she was cleaning the bathroom for a friend whose husband had just died. This lady did not look like a person who cleans very many bathrooms, and finding her on her knees in someone else's bath was a surprise. I asked her what was going on, and she told her story.

"My husband died without any warning. It seems incongruous that anyone would think of such a thing, but suddenly my house was full of people and I knew my bathroom was dirty. All afternoon I was in agony for fear someone would see that I was a messy housekeeper. I could not get it off my mind."

"I am not very good at knowing what to say to people when there is an illness or a death, so when I hear of someone's husband dying, I go to the house as soon as possible. I do not say much, I just hug the wife, and slip into the bathroom to give it a good cleaning. When I am through I hug the lady again and whisper, "The bathroom is clean, so don't worry."

Talk about TLC. This lady gives PPC—that stands for practical and personal care.

THE PRIEST WHO KNEW WHERE THE HELP WAS

At a meeting of suicide survivors, I heard a young mother tell of the suicide of her husband. It had not been long since the suicide had occurred, and the feelings were still raw and fresh. She told of all the people who came to give advice and counsel. She talked with bitterness about the ones who seemed to know exactly why the suicide happened, and even knew how God felt about it. Too often, in the real tragedies of life, someone comes to make the pain worse.

Then the lady smiled and said, "My priest helped me more than anyone else. He was so honest. He said he did not know why this happened, and had no idea how to console me. He told me he could not possibly know how I felt or what I feared. Then he said he did not know how to help, but he knew where the help was."

This priest had made it his business to investigate every helping agency in his city. He knew what each agency did, and how to make contact with them. He had personally met the heads of most of these agencies, and felt comfortable calling them for help. In this case he connected the lady with the suicide survivors group, and she found help among those who had been through what she was now experiencing.

The priest has tried to get every church group possible to explore all of the agencies, and to make a notebook of what each one is available to do. Sometimes the most help is to just know where help is.

The Catholic Diocese of Chicago has developed a concept called the Parish Nurse Program. As I understand it, these nurses are actively looking for people who need help. Most of their work is in connecting the folks with the agencies that give the kind of help needed. Often they find people who fall through the cracks of available help, and then they move to do much more than know where the help is. But, knowing where the help is may be the best part of this remarkable program.

THE CARE TEAM

I know three men who organized themselves into a unique type of care team. The group consists of a businessman, a lawyer, and an accountant. They make themselves available to any widow who needs financial consultation after the death of a husband.

They discovered that many widows have no idea about their husband's financial affairs, and suddenly are called upon to make massive decisions. These men do not take the place of accountants, lawyers, or any other service people. They are available to sit down with the widow and hear her fears and answer her questions. They find just letting her talk it out is often all the help she needs. They show her the options she has available, and help her sort out her thoughts enough to begin choosing between the options.

Their agreement is that none of them will let the widows they help become a client or pay anything for their services. This costs them some business. They all say there is no way they would trade the fullfillment they receive from helping for the business they miss.

THE COUPLE WHO KNOW

The insights some people have naturally without having the experience themselves often astounds me. I met a couple who have not suffered the death of a mate. They have not even gone through a serious illness. Without experience they figured out what it feels like to be a widow or widower in a world of couples.

Widows or widowers are suddenly single and do not fit in any world anymore. They are not single like the people in the singles groups that meet for fun and fellowship. They are no longer a couple, and feel like a fifth wheel at any gathering where couples go.

Often widows come to feel as if they threaten the wives of their friends. They find it hard to believe or accept that women they have loved and socialized with for years now shun them like they are something to be feared.

Widows find that couples will not come to their homes as couples. Often this is not because the wife now feels insecure or threatened, but because the husband does not know what to say. Usually the husband talked with the man when they were together, and he suddenly finds out he does not know how to talk with a woman he has known for years.

Widowers have a hard time finding anything except loneliness. There aren't as many widowers as there are widows, and they have a hard time making new friends. The old couples move on in their social lives. A new couple moves into the place the widower formerly occupied, and he feels replaced and lonely.

Both widows and widowers miss the contact with couples and the kinds of things couples do. That is the world they remember. That is the world they miss.

The couple in this story discovered this need and quietly moved to meet it. They simply invite widows and widowers to participate in their world. If they are going out to eat, they take someone with them. If there is an event where everyone goes as couples, they take a widow or two. They remind the old gang that the widows and widowers are still alive and need to be included. If an event excludes the widows and widowers, then this couple finds another event on the same night, and takes their little group out for a night of fun.

They have one cardinal rule: They never try to fix anyone up. They never invite males and females to events so they can meet. Playing Cupid is one need that is being taken care of by almost all of the friends and former friends. This couple is happy to leave the fixing up alone. They care enough to see a need and move to make it better.

THE ONES WHO WERE
THERE WHEN IT HAPPENED

I know a church group that decided the loneliest people in their city were the ones sitting in the emergency rooms of the hospitals. They organized themselves and asked the hospital to train them so they could be a help instead of a hindrance. They are in the emergency rooms at night when the most tragedies happen. They pour coffee and help the hospital with paper work. Mostly they listen to the stories of people in pain. They find ways to help we could not imagine.

One of the things they discovered was how much comfort they can be after a death. They visit the family the next day, and report how comfortable the family seems to be, and how easily they talk. Since these people were there when it happened, they seem like old friends to the family.

THE ONE WHO HEARS SCREAMS

I have a friend who specializes in the healing power of listening. She goes to the home after a death and says, "I do not know what to say to make the pain less intense, nor can I explain why this happened. A giant hole has been bitten out of your heart, and it will not grow back. You will learn to live with it. It will get better. Until it does get better, I want to be there for you. There will be nights when you need to call someone. You will not know what to say. You may just want to call and scream for awhile. Those are my nights. I will be there, and I want you to call."

A lady called my friend one night. The lady had suffered the death of a husband and a child, and she could barely talk. She said, "I am lying on the floor and I can't get up." My friend asked her what she felt like doing. The lady said, "I feel like screaming." My friend told her to go ahead and scream. The lady protested, of course, but finally began to scream. She screamed for what she must have thought was half an hour, but in reality was only a few minutes. Then she said, "Thank you I feel so much better," and hung up the phone.

My friend told me what a struggle she had learning to let people scream without thinking she had to say something. Now she has become the one who hears the screams, and in the process she gives practical and personal care.

THE ONE WHO REMEMBERS

Heroes are found in unexpected places. I found a shy little lady who has a hard time talking to people under the best of circumstances. She has an even harder time in times of crisis or grief. She says she is one of those who hangs around, hugs them, and hushes.

She has found a wonderful way to give practical and personal care. She remembers the anniversaries. She remembers the birthday of the person who died and the anniversary of the death. These are two of the hardest times for those in grief. This lady writes a little note that simply says she is thinking of the person during this time.

She remembers much longer than most would think necessary. She says the notes that do the most good are the ones for the fourth, fifth, and sixth anniversaries. The person in grief still hurts on these days and has no idea that anyone will still remember. But this shy little lady does, and her remembering helps.

THE INNOVATORS

There is no way for me to tell the stories of all of the innovative funeral directors I have met. These men and women have found unique ways to give practical and personal care.

The stories would cover the whole of the country. A funeral director in the Berkshires of New England discovered the need for significance and began structuring the visitation and funeral to honor the significance of each person. This man cares and shows it so much he has been called to come to adjoining states, not to conduct a funeral but to just be there with someone in grief.

Or the funeral director who decided not to hire

someone to direct the grief recovery groups. He hired someone to take his place at the funeral home, and directs the recovery groups and does the counseling himself.

Or the man who looks less like a funeral director than any one I know. His dress is sloppy at best, and his funerals may be the same. The people do not care. They know he loves them, so it does not matter how he dresses. He proves that people don't care how much we know, but they know how much we care.

I am glad this book did not finish before these stories where told. Often those who write the books or lead the groups or start national organizations are looked upon as the ones who do the most to help people walk through their grief. These things are important, but the real people who serve are the ones who dare to find a way to touch with practical and personal care.

Warm Fuzzies,
Doug Manning

Doug Manning

Doug Manning is the author of over twenty books designed to help people face the tough issues of life.

After thirty years as a minister and counselor, he began a new career almost twenty years ago as an author and speaker.

Doug has a warm conversational style in which he shares his insights from his various experiences. Contact In-Sight Books at 1-800-658-9262 for a complete catalog of his products or visit our website at www.insightbooks.com.

Selected Resources from In-Sight Books

When Love Gets Tough -
The Nursing Home Decision

Share My Lonesome Valley -
The Slow Grief of Long-term Care

Aging Is a Family Affair

Don't Take My Grief Away From Me

The Empty Chair -
The Journey of Grief After Suicide

The Special Care Series

Lean On Me Gently -
Helping The Grieving Child

I Know Someone Who Died coloring book

IN-SIGHT BOOKS, INC.